ASK
ABOUT

A
S
I
A

Mason Crest Publishers Inc.
370 Reed Road
Broomall, Pennsylvania 19008
(866) MCP-BOOK (toll free)

First printing

1 2 3 4 5 6 7 8 9 10

Library of Congress Cataloging-in-Publication Data on file at the Library of Congress.

ISBN 1-59084-200-6
ISBN 1-59084-198-0 (series)

Adapted from original concept produced by
Vineyard Freepress Pty Ltd, Sydney
Copyright © 1998 Vineyard Freepress Pty Ltd.

Project Editor	Valerie Hill
Text	Robin Morrow
Design	Denny Allnutt
Research	Peter Barker
Editor	Clare Booth
Cartography	Ray Sim
Consultants	Dorothy Minkoff, Alida Sijmons
Translation	Emi Murakawa
Images	Mike Langford, Japan National Tourist Organization, Consulate-General of Japan, The Japan Foundation, Japan Airlines, Valerie Hill, Ben Hill, Denny Allnutt, Canon Australia Pty Ltd, Kodansha International, National Gallery of Victoria, Sony Corporation, Suzuki Talent Association of Australia (NSW) Inc.

COVER: Huge lion mask ready for a procession.

TITLE PAGE: Paper-covered kite with heron design, as tall as a man.

CONTENTS: School girls climbing the active volcano, Mount Aso on Kyushu.

INTRODUCTION: Girls on their way to school in a Hokkaido winter.

Japan

MASON CREST PUBLISHERS

CONTENTS

THE LAND

A Crescent of Islands   8 – 9

Volcanoes and Earthquakes   10 – 11

THE NATION IS FORMED

Earliest Times   12 – 13

Nara and Heian-Kyo   14 – 15

Shoguns and Samurai   16 – 17

The Closed World of Edo   18 – 19

From Meiji to Modern   20 – 21

WAR AND RECONSTRUCTION

World War II   22 – 23

Rebuilding after the War   24 – 25

MODERN JAPAN

Government Today   26 – 27

Japan and the World   28 – 29

Farming and Fishing   30 – 31

Industry and Business   32 – 33

City of Tokyo   34 – 35

DAILY LIFE

Old and New   36 – 37

Family Life   38 – 39

Food for All Occasions   40 – 41

Education   42 – 43

Visiting Japan   44 – 45

Index and Picture Credits   46 – 47

INTRODUCTION

THE ISLAND NATION of Japan was cut off from the rest of the world for a long time. Traditions and skills passed from generation to generation to form a distinctive culture. Then the Japanese people showed that they were skillful also at learning what other societies had to offer. A time of expansion ended in the disasters of World War II.

The postwar rebuilding of Japan is a success story. From poverty and hunger, Japan rose to become a leader in technology and finance. A large population packed into a small area has benefited from being well organized and hard working. Young people growing up in Japan today are part of a society balanced delicately between the values and customs of tradition and modern, westernized ways.

A CRESCENT OF ISLANDS

▲ The Inland Sea.

Close to the northeastern coast of the Asian continent lies Japan. It is a country of hundreds of islands in the shape of a thin half moon about 1,862 miles from north to south. The four main islands in order of size are Honshu, Hokkaido, Kyushu and Shikoku. Two-thirds of Japan consists of mountains too steep for settlement or for farming. People live mainly in cities that have sprung up on the flat lowlands. Japan is one of the most densely populated countries in the world. You are never far from the sea in Japan: on the east is the Pacific Ocean and on the west, separating Japan from Korea, is the Sea of Japan. Temperatures range from –40°F in the icy winters of the north to summer temperatures of 85°F, often with high humidity.

Seasons in Japan are:
haru   spring (March to May)
natsu summer (June to August)
aki   autumn (September to November)
fuyu   winter (December to February)

THE SEASONS

As well as the four seasons, the Japanese have a special word for a time when the monsoon brings much rain: *tsuyu*. This extra season lasts from mid-June to mid-July.

▼ Nagoya is typical of city growth in mountainous Japan. Plains such as these were formerly used for agriculture.

The seasons play an important part in many aspects of life. In traditional clothing there are different patterns for *obi* or sashes: for example, in spring plum blossoms, and in autumn red maple leaves. The weather is dependable. Cherry blossom appears in Tokyo between late March and early April. An outing to view and enjoy the blossoms, as the children in the picture are doing, is called *hanami*. Because the weather in Japan turns very cold suddenly, the autumn leaves are spectacular and people go on outings to view these too.

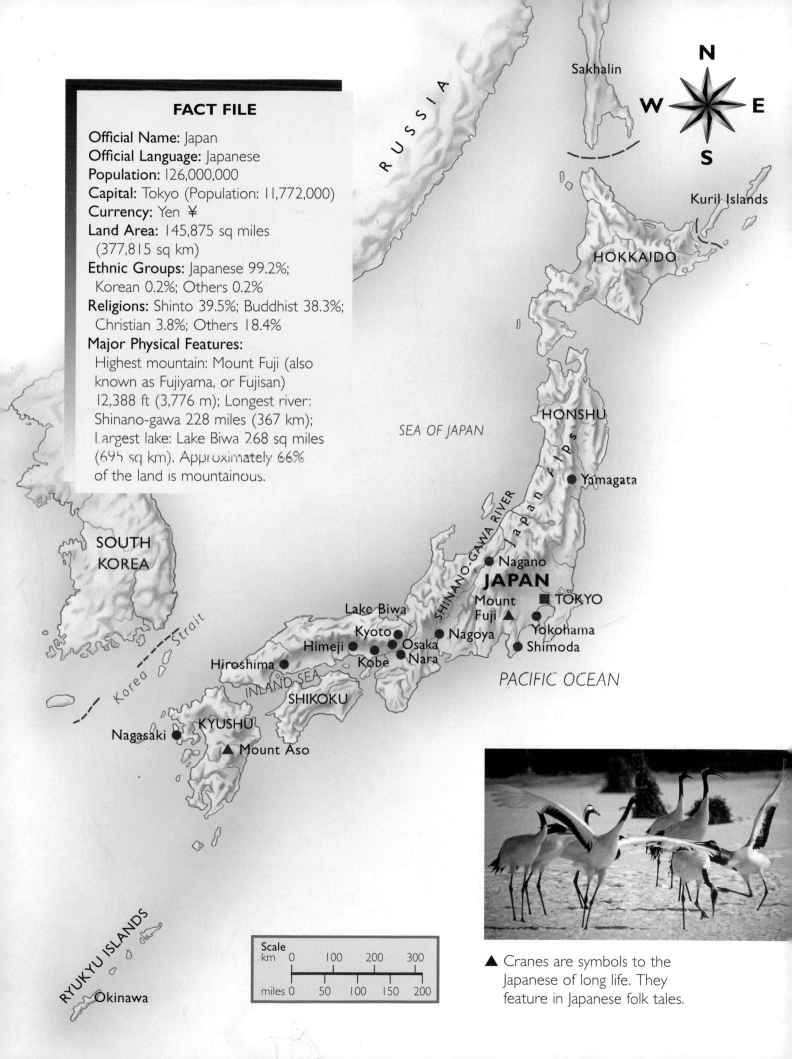

FACT FILE

Official Name: Japan
Official Language: Japanese
Population: 126,000,000
Capital: Tokyo (Population: 11,772,000)
Currency: Yen ¥
Land Area: 145,875 sq miles
(377,815 sq km)
Ethnic Groups: Japanese 99.2%;
Korean 0.2%; Others 0.2%
Religions: Shinto 39.5%; Buddhist 38.3%;
Christian 3.8%; Others 18.4%
Major Physical Features:
Highest mountain: Mount Fuji (also
known as Fujiyama, or Fujisan)
12,388 ft (3,776 m); Longest river:
Shinano-gawa 228 miles (367 km);
Largest lake: Lake Biwa 268 sq miles
(695 sq km). Approximately 66%
of the land is mountainous.

Sakhalin

Kuril Islands

RUSSIA

HOKKAIDO

HONSHU

SEA OF JAPAN

Japan Alps

Yamagata

Nagano

JAPAN

Mount
Fuji ▲ ■ TOKYO

Yokohama

Shimoda

Lake Biwa

Kyoto

Nagoya

SHINANO-GAWA RIVER

SOUTH
KOREA

Himeji

Osaka

Kobe Nara

Hiroshima

PACIFIC OCEAN

Korea Strait

INLAND SEA

SHIKOKU

KYUSHU

Nagasaki

▲ Mount Aso

RYUKYU ISLANDS

Okinawa

Scale
km 0   100   200   300

miles 0   50   100   150   200

▲ Cranes are symbols to the
Japanese of long life. They
feature in Japanese folk tales.

VOLCANOES AND EARTHQUAKES

The mountainous islands that make up Japan were shaped by volcanoes and earthquakes. There are at least 40 active volcanoes and many dormant ones in Japan today. The country experiences thousands of earthquakes every year. Most do little damage, but about once each century there is a massive earthquake. In 1923, the Great Tokyo Earthquake caused many fires and the loss of more than 100,000 lives. During 1995, the worst earthquake in Japan for 70 years hit the port city of Kobe. Five thousand people were killed and 56,000 buildings destroyed or damaged. When an earthquake shakes the ocean floor it can result in tidal waves, or *tsunami,* which cause great damage when they strike land.

▲ Crater of Mount Aso, an active volcano.

▼ *The Wave,* of *tsunami* proportions, is a famous color woodcut, or *ukiyo.*
Katsushika Hokusai
1760–1849 Japan
The Hollow of the Deep-Sea Wave off Kanagawa, c.1830
Color woodcut, 10 × 14.6 in
Felton Bequest 1909
National Gallery of Victoria, Melbourne

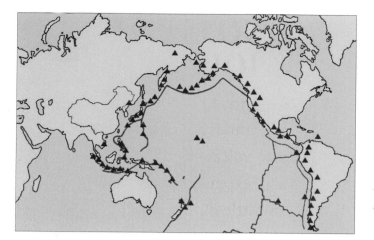

RING OF FIRE

This map shows that Japan is part of a volcanic chain which encircles the Pacific Ocean. Sometimes called the Ring of Fire, the volcanic chain follows the fault lines between tectonic plates of the earth's crust. Movement of these plates results in earthquakes and the formation of volcanoes. Hot spot volcanoes occur away from the fault lines. The vent of a volcano allows gas and molten rock to rise up to the surface of the earth. Molten rock cools to form the conical shape of a volcano and provides fertile soil. Volcanoes can be active or dormant (inactive).

EARTHQUAKE

An English poet, James Kirkup, who lived in Japan for fifteen years, described his experience of an earthquake in poetic form:

*I notice that all the telegraph poles
  along the lane
Are wagging convulsively, and the wires
Bounce like skipping-ropes round
  flustered birds.
The earth creeps under the floor.*

Earthquake, James Kirkup (1923–)

▲ An earthquake simulator teaches people about storing belongings and sheltering during a tremor or a quake. At school and at work people are taught how to protect themselves and help others.

▼ Emergency support teams clearing debris. Scientists monitor seismic activity and the community is highly organized for emergencies —even small children learn fire drill.

▲ Mount Fuji. This dormant volcano, the highest mountain in the country, is seen by the Japanese as a symbol of the beauty of their land. It is believed that everyone should climb it at least once in a lifetime.

▲ Pottery figurine of the Jomon period.

EARLIEST TIMES

The Jomon people, hunting and gathering in the natural environment, were the first to occupy the Japanese islands. In about 400 BC, the Yayoi came from the Asian mainland. With them they brought the skill of growing rice in flooded fields. This practice has been vital in the development of Japan. By the fifth century AD a small nation formed around present-day Nara. Warriors of this time and up to AD 650, the Kofun period, rode horses and carried iron swords and bows.

▲ Massive rice straw rope, a *shimenawa,* divides the "purified" inside of a Shinto shrine from the "unclean" outside world.

▼ Raincoat of woven rice straw, or *mino.*

▶ Pottery dog dating from the Kofun period.

▼ Rice fields under water, a method of cultivation which has been used in Japan for about 2,400 years.

▲ Ainu men in traditional costume. The Ainu people, who now live mostly in the north, are believed to be descended from the original Jomon people.

The sun has always had a special place in Japanese culture. The ancient Chinese, seeing the sun rise over islands to the east, called them *ji-pen*, or "source of the sun." Yamato emperors claimed the Sun Goddess as their ancestor. The Japanese now call their land *Nippon*, "Land of the Rising Sun." The sun disc, called *Hinomaru*, is used as the Japanese flag (below left).

SHINTO

Shinto is the ancient religion of Japan. People believed that powerful spirits, or *kami*, inhabited millions of sacred places such as trees or mountains. As Shinto developed, ancestors and heroes were added to the *kami*. Most important of all was *Amaterasu Omikami*, the Sun Goddess. Her shrine at Ise is still the most sacred place in Japan. Today some people have a "god shelf" at home where food is offered to the spirits.

▲ Shrines where Shinto believers worship are marked by a *Torii* gate, which was originally designed as a roost for birds brought for sacrifice to the gods.

◀ In a fiery ritual, wooden prayer chips are burned by Shinto priests. They teach that the smoke carries the prayers up to heaven.

NARA AND HEIAN-KYO

Many ideas which influenced the Japanese way of life were brought across the sea from China and Korea. Chinese laws, government, and writing were adopted into Japanese culture. The teachings of Buddhism arrived in the sixth century AD and by the time Nara became the capital in AD 710, the emperor and nobles were Buddhist. Emperor Kammu built a model city in the eighth century and named it *Heian-Kyo*, "capital of peace and tranquillity."

▲ The Gion Festival was first held in Kyoto in the ninth century. It began, they say, in the hope that the gods would halt an epidemic raging at the time. Some of the beautifully decorated floats can hold a full orchestra. Most festivals began as religious celebrations, such as in autumn, thanking the gods for the harvest. Shinto and Buddhist customs combine in some festivals. Today festivals are a time to dress in special costumes and have fun.

KANJI

Kanji, one of three kinds of Japanese characters, are based on those developed by the Chinese. *Kanji* are signs, or pictographs, telling the meaning of a word. *Kanji* were originally written with a brush and ink called *sumi*, which is made from soot and glue. There is a correct order for placing the brush strokes. Master calligraphers say that not just your hand but your whole body and mind need to work together to make beautiful writing.

These *kanji* are the signs for **person** and **tree**.

人 + 木 = 休

Together they mean "**rest**."

◄ Calligraphy tools.

Later the name was changed to Kyoto. This city was the capital of Japan for a thousand years. It had straight roads and a system of canals. The Heian court was known for its literature, elegance, and beauty. Kyoto is still a center of arts and crafts such as scroll painting and sculpture.

Techniques for working with metal, wood, bamboo, and paper have been handed down from master to pupil.

◀ Hand-crafted doll shows a young woman of the aristocracy wearing the *junihitoe*, a twelve-layered court robe of the Heian period (AD 800–1200).

◀ Five-stringed Japanese lute from the eighth century.

BUDDHISM

When Buddhism was brought from China it formed links with the old religion of Shinto. Often a Buddhist temple would be built on the site of a Shinto shrine. Nowadays many Japanese have Buddhist funerals, and ancestors are honored at Buddhist altars. The title Buddha means "enlightened one." Gautama Siddhartha (about 500 BC) was a wealthy Indian prince who, shocked to discover the suffering of the world, left his life of luxury to seek enlightenment. He taught his followers about the Four Noble Truths and the Noble Eight-fold Path. There are many different kinds of Buddhism—the Japanese later developed Zen, a particularly disciplined form.

▲ *Daibutsu*, a huge eighth century bronze and gold image of Buddha in the Todaiji Temple, Nara.

▶ An eighth century marquetry box found at Horyuji Temple at Nara. Built first in AD 607, this temple claims the oldest wooden buildings in the world.

SHOGUNS AND SAMURAI

The medieval period was an age of war and warriors. Japan's first *shogun*, or army commander-in-chief, was Minamoto Yoritomo. As the power of the *shoguns* grew, the influence of the emperors weakened. The *shogun* ruled over powerful warlords called *daimyo*, whose armed followers were called *samurai*, meaning "ones who serve," or *bushi*, the "fighting men." They lived by a strict code of honor known as the Way of the Warrior, or *bushido*.

▲ Himeji Castle was also called the White Heron.

▼ *Samurai* warfare is reenacted at the Uesugi Festival.

◄ Mask used in *Noh*, the oldest type of Japanese theater. Words, music, and dance combine to tell a story in this stylized art

◀ Procession of mounted bowmen, dressed as in medieval times.

ZEN AND THE TEA CEREMONY

Zen is a form of Buddhism that teaches that the way to enlightenment is through training and meditation. A Zen priest lives by begging for food and money. Everyday life in Japan is influenced by Zen, with its emphasis on carrying out activities in the simple but correct way.

During the mid-fifteenth century, the country was torn apart by civil war. From the sixteenth century, a series of powerful leaders began to reunify the nation. The first direct contact with Europe came in 1543. Portuguese ships brought firearms, trade, and Roman Catholic missionaries. However, the government later became worried about foreign ideas and forbade missionary teaching.

Today in Japan you can take part in a tea ceremony just as it was perfected in the sixteenth century— but you must not be in a rush! The "way of tea" is based on Zen ideas of discipline and simplicity. Every detail is important. The host ladles powdered green tea into each cup, pours hot water over it, and stirs it with a whisk. The guest must bow, receive the tea bowl, and rotate it before drinking.

▼ *Samurai* armor was made from lacquered leather and metal.

▼ The gardens of Zen temples are designed to give a feeling of tranquillity. A stone may stand for a whole mountain; white sand may represent flowing water.

◀ Teahouses are built for the ceremony. They usually have a simple garden and low doorway so you must humble yourself to enter. There is a waiting room, a room for up to five guests to be served, and a room to wash the utensils. The Japanese word *wabi* describes the beauty of such simple design.

THE CLOSED WORLD OF EDO

Under the rule of the *shoguns* Japan became virtually isolated from the outside world for more than 250 years. During this time, the *shoguns* became even more powerful. The turning point in Japanese history came at the battle of Sekighara in AD 1600, when the most powerful warlord, Tokugawa Ieyasu, gained control over the whole country. The emperor made him *shogun*. He ruled from the castle town of Edo, which rapidly grew into a city. The *shogun* controlled his warlords by requiring them and their families to spend time in Edo. Cut off from the rest of the world, and with stability in the regions, Edo became a center of leisure and art.

▲ *Bunraku* puppets are over half life-size. The puppeteers wear black and are seen on stage. ▼

▼ Moats and high walls surrounded castles.

▼ Bamboo staves are used in *Kendo* training today; *samurai* trained mind and body in these skills.

▲ *Kabuki* drama.

While the warlords and their followers were in Edo, much of their time was spent in entertainment and the arts. The period became famous for the vitality of its drama and puppetry. Many woodcuts created at the time, such as Hokusai's picture of a great wave (page 10), are considered masterpieces. This city of elegant castles, moats, and gardens eventually became Tokyo.

▲ *Geisha* painted their faces white and wore elaborate kimonos. They were skilled in singing, dancing, conversing, and poetry.

▼ Kintai Bridge, Honshu.

▼ The last *shogun* returned power to the emperor. *The Restoration of Imperial Rule* (12 October 1867).

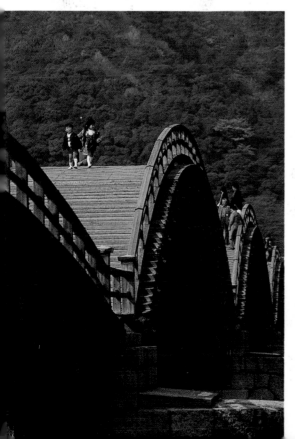

FROM MEIJI TO MODERN

▲ Edo was renamed Tokyo, or "eastern capital." The painting above shows the young Meiji emperor moving from Kyoto to Tokyo in October 1868. The old manner of travel and dress was still used.

During the nineteenth and twentieth centuries, massive changes took place in Japan. The old ways of *daimyo* and *samurai* were swept aside and industrial modernization, modeled on western countries, was introduced. In 1854 the arrival of steam ships from America—Commodore Perry's "black ships"—ended Japan's 250 years of isolation from the rest of the world. Japan had to agree to trade with the United States and later with other countries. There was also political and social reform. Powerful *daimyo* rose up against the *shogun* and brought an end to the Edo period. In 1868, the rule of the Meiji emperor was restored.

▲ The Black Ships Festival is held each year at Shimoda.

▶ Women and children wearing western dress at Rockumeikan Hall, where leaders of fashion adopted the styles of western diplomats. Meiji officials were sent to study western countries and returned with ideas for modernizing industry and many aspects of life.

◀ Japanese troops march toward Shantung, China (1927 and 1928). Before World War II, Japan had occupied part of China, Korea, Sakhalin, and Taiwan, as can be seen on the map on page 22.

When Emperor Hirohito ascended the throne in 1926 he took the name *Showa* or "enlightenment and harmony," but his reign was to be filled with conflict and war. During a time of poverty in the 1920s and 1930s, Japanese army and navy leaders took control of the government, pushing to expand the empire. They invaded China and Korea and set up colonies, which they ruled harshly. When British and American opinion turned against Japan, Japan joined with Germany and Italy at the beginning of World War II.

ADAPTING WESTERN IDEAS

▲ Changes included introduction of electricity, trains and trams, elections and a public education system.

◀ Japanese and western artists were interested in each others' art forms. This sculpture, *Foot Tricks*, 1914, by Tobari Kogan, shows a western influence.

◀ The *Kamikaze*. This early airplane attempted a world record between Tokyo and London in 1937. It was named for a "divine wind" that drove back invading Mongol ships in the thirteenth century. The Japanese saw this wind as the gods defending their country. They applied the same word, *kamikaze*, late in World War II to pilots who crashed their planes, loaded with explosives, into enemy targets.

WORLD WAR II

For many years Japan had occupied neighboring countries. When the war-minded General Tojo became prime minister in 1941, Japan also occupied Indochina (now Vietnam). The United States then cut off Japanese oil supplies. In December 1941 Japan attacked and destroyed almost all the U.S. Pacific Fleet at Pearl Harbor, Hawaii. The United States declared war on Japan, and so World War II reached the Pacific region. At first, Japan had many victories—in the Philippines, Indonesia, Malaysia, Singapore, and Burma. In 1945 the United States retaliated by dropping atom bombs on the Japanese cities of Hiroshima and Nagasaki. Soon after this, Emperor Hirohito broadcast a speech in which he gave his decision to surrender.

▲ Aerial photo of the Japanese attack on the U.S. Pacific Fleet at Pearl Harbor, 8 December 1941.

▲ Japanese soldiers advance into Thailand and Burma in 1942. Captured Allied soldiers and other prisoners were forced by the Japanese to work in terrible conditions building the Burma railway. Japanese traditionally believed that it was shameful to be captured, so they treated prisoners harshly. There were many thousands of deaths.

▶ The yellow line shows Japanese conquests before World War II, the orange line the greatest extent of Japanese conquests during World War II.

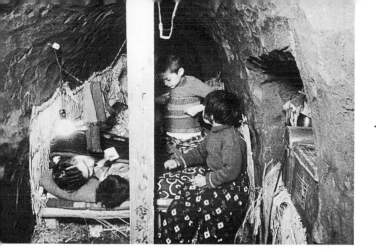

◀ Inside an air raid shelter. Japan had been at war for so many years that people at home suffered food shortages and poor living conditions. Everyone worked for the war effort.

▶ School children at military training.

◀ Women volunteers made war supplies.

THE WAR ENDS

During World War II, scientists on both sides worked frantically to develop an atom bomb. U.S. scientists demonstrated their success in August 1945 in Japan. The atom bomb was the most destructive weapon the world had seen until then. The Hiroshima and Nagasaki bombs killed more than 100,000 people and wounded as many more. Many deaths were slow, as a result of exposure to radiation. Some people believe Japan would soon have surrendered even if the bombs were not used; others say that dropping the bombs prevented more deaths from a continuing war.

▲ Atomic bombing of Hiroshima on 6 August 1945.

▶ Representatives of the Allied forces and the Japanese people and armed forces at the surrender ceremony aboard *USS Missouri* on 2 September 1945.

REBUILDING AFTER THE WAR

While Japanese forces were fighting the war in the Asia Pacific region, people at home in Japan suffered hunger and poverty. Their cities were bombed and burned. Added to this, after the surrender, tens of thousands of Japanese came flooding back from other countries, needing food, housing, and jobs. A huge task faced Japan. Under a postwar agreement, General Douglas MacArthur and Allied officials, mostly American, supplied resources and worked with Japanese people to rebuild the country. The Peace Constitution states that the Japanese people "forever renounce war." It allowed Japan to keep a military force for defense only. A Bill of Rights was introduced, and the country started rebuilding as a modern nation. The Japanese accepted the help they were given and resumed control of their changed society. Because of its vigorous growth, Japan was soon known as a "tiger economy."

▲ *Origami* paper cranes, like the ones Sadako and her friends make in the famous story, *Sadako and the Thousand Paper Cranes*, by Eleanor Coerr. The book tells of a girl suffering from leukemia after the Hiroshima bombing. She believes that a thousand paper cranes will save her life.

◄ A shattered dome left standing in the rubble of Hiroshima after atomic bombing.

▼ Peace Memorial Park, with the dome kept as a memorial and reminder of the terrible results of war. Hiroshima, rebuilt, is now a modern city with parks and trees.

▲ Roads and high-rise buildings were constructed as cities were rebuilt.

Meantime, life was hard. During and after the war there were serious food shortages, as most supplies had been sent to the soldiers. In rebuilding Japan, restoration of medical care and food supply received early attention.

▲ Planting vegetable seeds in bomb sites. People could not get enough rice so they cooked the potatoes and pumpkins which they grew.

▶ A school lunch system was organized.

▼ Land was reclaimed and farm machinery introduced. This grain is being harvested on land which had once been a swamp.

ひとつめあたら しいだいよう食 てもつくろかな

つくって

…Next, add grated potato and minced dried sardines…

つぎにおいもの きりくすやニボシ のくすを°いれます
……

Finally, add rice husks, and mix well.

さいごに ヌカをいれ よくかきまぜます

That was the recipe for chicken feed.

ただいまは ニワトリの えさについて もうしあげました

▲ The cartoon character Sazae-san first appeared just after the war and helped to lighten up the hard times. This cartoon shows Sazae listening to a recipe on the radio for making do with the poor quality "substitute" food of the time.

▶ Kitchen appliances and precooked food of the 1960s.

GOVERNMENT TODAY

The constitution drawn up in 1946 stated that Japan was to be a parliamentary democracy. All Japanese people over the age of twenty have the right to vote. They elect representatives to the national parliament, known as the Diet. There are two houses of parliament, the lower house, or House of Representatives, and the upper house, or House of Councillors. The head of government is the prime minister.

▲▶
Exterior and interior of the Diet building.

The leader is chosen from the party that the people elect to power. A governor heads each of the country's 47 divisions, or "prefectures." In this form of constitutional monarchy, the emperor is a figurehead with no governmental power.

◀ The chrysanthemum, symbol of the imperial family, serves as the national emblem of Japan, which unlike many other countries, does not have a coat-of-arms.

THE EMPEROR

The longest reign of a Japanese emperor ended in 1989 with the death of Emperor Hirohito, who had seen amazing changes in his lifetime. The next year, Emperor Akihito became the first emperor appointed under the postwar constitution. Early emperors, looked upon as gods, remained separate from the people. Today, the emperor is the symbol of the state and of the unity of the people.

The respect and affection of the people for their emperor unites them as a nation.

▲ Emperor Akihito, dressed informally at a rice harvest ceremony. He is no longer regarded as a divine descendant of the gods, and moves among the people.

◀ Emperor Akihito and his family.

Members of the parliament are elected by ballot. There are lower levels of government in cities, villages, and towns, where voting takes place. The government has to deal with Japan's large population, which has increased from about 72 million in 1940, to 126 million in the late 1990s. Organizing such a large population in a small land area is a demanding task.

▲ Women were first granted the right to vote in December 1945.

◀ The government builds efficient transport systems. Seto Ohashi bridge links the islands of Honshu and Shikoku across the Inland Sea.

▼ Japanese forces in a ceremonial parade. The constitution of 1946 states that "the Japanese people forever renounce war as a sovereign right of the nation." So although a wealthy and important country, Japan has a small military force, of volunteers, and depends for security on its alliance with the United States.

▲ The government of Japan manages its complex import and export economy. For example, shipbuilding, car manufacture, and the seagoing expertise of Japan's merchant navy combine to export cars to ports around the world.

JAPAN AND THE WORLD

There has been great exchange of ideas between Japan and other countries. From the late eighteenth century, when western countries established trade with Japan, a "cult of Japan" in Europe influenced the design of fabrics, pottery, and printing. Since then, Japanese style, with its clean lines and open spaces, has been taken into many art forms, including architecture, landscape gardening, and flower arranging. For their part, Japanese businesses have developed international ideas and products, and individuals have adopted western dress and lifestyle—in the home, people sit on chairs as well as on traditional floor cushions; when they go out, young people wear jeans, eat fast food, and listen to western music.

▲ Ivory *geisha* figurine. Artifacts like this were brought home by soldiers and civilians returning to their countries after helping rebuild Japan in the 1950s.

◄ Dr. Suzuki demonstrates his method of learning to play a violin. Children all around the world learn music by the Suzuki method. They can also take piano and organ lessons, usually starting at the age of two or three years.

私の一句

Sand for a mattress
so peaceful in the hot sun
waves swallow my feet

砂がマットレス
暑い太陽を浴びてとても平和だ
波が足をあらっていく

HAIKU

A poem in a World Haiku Contest organized by Japan Airlines. This *haiku* was written by Talia Jane Verhaaf, of South Australia, at the age of 12. *Haiku* written by children from around the world, in their own languages, were published in *Haiku by the Children*.

Do you know how to write a *haiku*? It is a very short poem about nature, with the essence of something the writer has seen or felt, usually including a word expressing a season of the year. The set pattern of syllables is 5–7–5. A good *haiku* has a "point of surprise" near the end. *Haiku* were part of an old form of linked verse, but Shiki Masaoka (1867–1902) gave them much of their present form.

SONY, A JAPANESE SUCCESS STORY

Two ex-navy men founded the Tokyo Communications Industrial company in 1945 in a bombed-out building in a suburb of Tokyo. By 1956 this struggling company had devised a way of using transistors, which had been invented in the United States, to build a tiny radio, which they named Sony. The radios were distributed in the United States, and Sony became one of the most famous names of the twentieth century. Sony produced the Walkman (above) in 1979 and CD player in 1982, world firsts. Automobile manufacturers Toyota and Honda, two other big exporters, started in a similarly modest way.

▶ Another tiny gadget that has become a world seller is the *Tamagotchi*.

◀ Japan is involved with the rest of the world in aid projects. This Japanese doctor is part of a Red Cross medical team that assists other countries during disaster and famine.

▲ Ready for their *karate* class, these boys are learning a martial art that began in medieval times. One-to-one combat sports that have spread from Japan around the world also include *judo* and the oldest martial art, *kendo*, which is based on the swordsmanship of the *samurai*. In turn, Japan has adopted western sports with enthusiasm—golf, baseball, ▼ and soccer are favorites.

▼ A *shishiodoshi* is a length of bamboo carefully balanced so that water trickles into it from a spout above. When it is full, the weight of the water tips and empties the bamboo pipe. Then it swings back and the pipe strikes a rock, making a hollow sound originally meant to frighten animals from the garden.

FARMING AND FISHING

Agriculture began in Japan about 2,000 years ago with the growing of rice. Only about 14 percent of Japan's land is suitable for farming. Rice is grown in traditional flooded fields. But now seedlings are transplanted from seedbeds into fields by machine, not by hand. Modern Japanese farms are very small, on average 3.5 acres. In this country, which is people-rich but space-poor, it is important that farmers grow as much as possible in small areas. Most farms are family owned, but the family usually has some income other than farming. Japanese fishing fleets harvest the oceans.

▲ Winter stock feed, such as baled lucerne hay, is imported. Canada is a major supplier. Livestock are housed and fed in barns because of the cold winters and shortage of grazing land.

▶ Poultry are kept in batteries of cages to force higher egg production.

▼ Hay is stored in a barn for the cold winter months.

▼ Lot-fed cattle are kept in small pens and fed daily by the farmer.

▲ Farmlands are snow covered during northern winters.

▲ Terraced rice fields on the island of Shikoku.

▲ Melon growing in a hot house. More than half the fruit and vegetables the Japanese need are grown in their own country. Customers insist on fresh, high-quality products.

▶ Ripe barley crop ready for harvesting in Hokkaido.

FOOD FROM THE SEA

Japanese people eat more seafood per person than those of any other nation in the world. Fleets of fishing boats go out daily to fish the coastal waters, but fish stocks are diminishing, especially where there is pollution. Some people in other countries disapprove of the way Japanese fishing boats driftnet the sea. Seafood is now imported from other countries. Huge quantities of fish, shellfish, and seaweed are grown in freshwater and coastal aquaculture farms.

◀ Fish farming.

▶ Squid drying in the sun.

INDUSTRY AND BUSINESS

The wealth of Japan is built upon very limited natural resources. Japan's greatest strength is the Japanese people, who are a highly educated and skilled workforce. Manufacturing industries export finished products in exchange for much-needed oil, minerals, and raw materials; imports supply over 90 percent of Japan's need for coal, iron ore, copper, and lead. Since the 1970s, Japan's efforts have been directed to high-technology industries. Government and private business cooperate in this development.

▲ Japan has become an exporting country, sending goods to countries all over the world. Japanese companies also build factories overseas.

DOING BUSINESS IN JAPAN

Business dealings in Japan are based on personal respect and trust and begin with exchange of cards and a respectful bow. Japanese business people take time to get to know each other. Companies take a long term view, working for steady growth and market share. Employers treat workers well and expect total commitment to the company.

Japanese companies invest for the future, and people are in the habit of saving. But Japan depends heavily on world trade, and is affected by the financial stability of other countries. If the value of Japan's currency, the yen (¥), falls, it has a great effect on trading partners.

▲ Osaka branch of the Bank of Japan.

◄ The Tokyo Stock Exchange, where shares in businesses are bought and sold, became one of the busiest in the world. The success of Japanese companies, in good times, gives the yen a high exchange value. This means Japanese people have more money to spend.

As they have done for centuries, the Japanese adopt and develop ideas from other countries. Japan is a world leader in technology, including satellites, electronics, and computers. The personal stereo, compact disc, and *Tamagotchi* were all invented in Japan, which is now one of the wealthiest nations in the world.

▲ Japanese weather satellite relays information to many countries.

▲ The Canon ELPH camera.

▶ Robots at work on an automated production line that assembles cars.

▼ Japan is a leader in medical and biochemical research.

▼ Japanese-built tankers carry oil supplies for industry.

CITY OF TOKYO

Tokyo is a busy, prosperous city. It was the center of culture during the Edo period and has been the capital of Japan since 1868. Twice during the twentieth century Tokyo was almost completely destroyed, first by the Great Tokyo Earthquake of 1923 and later by fire bombing during World War II. Rebuilding has resulted in a city that combines the historic with the ultramodern. At the center is the Imperial Palace, which is surrounded by moats and gardens. The city has many shrines and parks. Soaring multistory office blocks crowd either side of narrow streets. Along with museums and art galleries, you can find sports and entertainment centers, such as golf driving ranges, baseball batting cages, and noisy computer game halls.

▲ Each year Boys' Day is celebrated. Many boys dress in the traditional costume and carry a *samurai* sword.

▼ Fireworks over the Sumida River.

▲ The Ginza, Tokyo's famous shopping district, with restaurants, bazaars, and stores displaying the best of the world's fashion.

▶ Souvenir shops. Tokyo streets are clean despite the huge crowds.

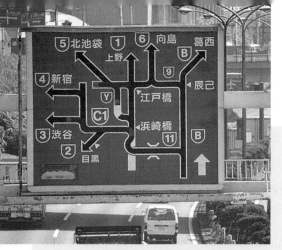

TRAFFIC IN TOKYO

About one-tenth of the population of Japan lives in the Tokyo Prefecture. Many commuters travel long distances to work. Traffic jams are a fact of life in the capital, and it is very hard to find a parking space. Electronic traffic signs guide motorists away from congested areas. The underground railway, with ten crisscrossing lines, is efficient but overloaded. Maps with the lines coded and signs in English are helpful to visitors.

▲ Shinjuku office tower.

▼ Bicycles wait at suburban stations for commuters, who joke, "The last person off the train at night rides home on the worst bicycle."

▲ A *koban*, or police box. Police are stationed on many corners. They help with directions and lost property as well as watch for crime.

◄ Asakusa Kannon Buddhist temple, with its huge paper lantern, has been rebuilt many times on the same site since the seventh century.

▼ The White Heron Dance was performed at Asakusa temple to celebrate the centenary of Tokyo's restoration as capital by the Meiji emperor.

OLD AND NEW

▲ *Shinkansen*, or bullet trains, were introduced in 1964 for the Tokyo Olympics. These trains are so fast the scenery outside becomes a blur. The first line followed the old Tokkaido route south from Tokyo; you can see Mount Fuji from trains on this line.

In the second half of the twentieth century, Japan is using the most up-to-date technology in daily life. Modern devices simplify communication, travel, work, and entertainment. This new technology sits like an overlay on centuries-old customs. Many inventions solve old problems, among them improving fire fighting techniques and making tall buildings stable during earthquakes. Music, theater, and sports often show traces of old customs. Shinto shrines are found in the corners of bustling cities. Even the bullet train from Tokyo to Kyoto follows the route of medieval processions.

▲ The beckoning cat is used as a decoration for shops as it is thought to attract customers. Rounded *daruma* dolls are believed to make wishes come true and are popular with election candidates.

Buildings of concrete and steel with electric lighting are safer than the old wooden buildings and paper lanterns. Fires were so common in old Tokyo, especially after earthquakes, that they were called "the flowers of Edo."

▲ Paper lanterns, now used for festivals and decorations, once lighted homes.

◀ Electric and neon lighting has reduced the risk of fire.

▶ Robotic fire engine. This invention allows fire fighting at close quarters without risk to human life.

MANGA

Comics, or *manga*, are based on a traditional style of drawing. Now they are mostly published weekly in thick books. Adults as well as children rush to buy the latest issue. One of the most popular *manga* characters of all time was *Atomu* (Astro Boy), shown above right with his creator, Tezuka Osamu.

▼ In the ancient sport of *sumo* wrestling, a bout begins with scattering salt to purify the ring.

▲ Rock band Dreams Come True. Japanese traditional music and western classical music are popular. Performers and listeners enjoy international jazz, blues, and rock, as well as Japanese-style *kayokyuku*, which is based on the distinctive Japanese scale.

◄ The *koto* is a thirteen-stringed instrument. The right hand plucks the strings while the left hand presses the strings behind the bridge to alter the tone.

◄ After reading their fortunes at a Shinto shrine, these girls will hang the slips of paper as prayers on lines with many others. Few Japanese people now follow Shinto beliefs, but they keep some customs such as wedding rituals and New Year ceremonies.

FAMILY LIFE

The extended family, which included grandparents and other relatives, has given way to small family units, often of parents and only one child. The father works long hours and is often expected to eat and drink with business associates after work. The mother manages the home and family affairs, giving great attention to the children's upbringing and education. Now, she often also seeks employment outside the home, so the "latch key" child has become common in Tokyo. However, children are much loved in Japan, and are usually fully provided for by parents who are both employed.

▲ A Shinto wedding ceremony includes taking sips of *sake*, or Japanese rice wine. Many couples have a western-style ceremony as well. Marriages used to be arranged between families with the help of a matchmaker, or *nakodo*, but today most young people choose their own marriage partner.

▶ Japanese housewives shop daily for fresh ingredients they will use to prepare meals at home.

▶ This grandmother works in the fishing industry.

▶ Family members pay respect at ancestors' graves.

◀ Snapshot of a farming family in the rural area near Nagano. Although the plant nursery run by this family is highly organized, their lifestyle is more relaxed than that of city families. Rural families also tend to be larger than city families.

◀ A meal in a restaurant is an accepted way to combine business with relaxation. The men sit on cushions. A wall alcove, or *toconoma*, displays decorative objects.

▲ In the family, children learn to wear traditional dress, respect older people, observe rules for bowing and use polite forms of language and table manners.

HOMES AND LIFESTYLE

The lifestyle in Japan has been shaped by the large numbers of people living in this small country. People must live and work close to one another. Most city people occupy very small apartments with little space to ask people home for meals, so they eat out and spend time outdoors.

Traditional ways of overcoming shortage of space are still used. In old-style houses, only a paper sliding screen separated rooms, so a code of behavior was developed to allow privacy—rather like pretending that no one else was there! Now homes and apartments usually have solid walls and doors, but the privacy of others is still respected.

People like to have a garden, even if it is "no bigger than a cat's forehead." An art form that meets this need is *bonsai*—tiny gardens in pots with trees grown and pruned to keep them small.

▲ Village housing, Shikoku Island.

▼▶ Crowds of young people throng city shops and amusements, and also enjoy open space on a beachcombing trip to a quiet beach.

FOOD FOR ALL OCCASIONS

Rice, seafood, and vegetables make up the traditional healthy diet of the Japanese people. Rice is so important that the words for the main meal times all include *gohan*, the word for rice. About one hundred years ago meat was added. Now Japanese food includes beef dishes, such as *sukiyaki*, and chicken dishes like the popular *yakitori*, which is cooked on skewers. Japanese people shop daily for food, as they like it to be as fresh as possible, especially the raw fish used in *sashimi* and *sushi*. Soy beans are used for *miso* soup, soy sauce, and *tofu*. Noodles in a bowl of soup are lunch time favorites. The most common drink is green tea, or *o-cha*.

▲ *Bento*, or box meals, are sold in many places, especially railway stations. The food, neatly packed in compartments, usually includes rice and local specialities.

Say it in JAPANESE!
breakfast – *asa gohan*
lunch – *hiru gohan*
dinner – *ban gohan*

▲ Roadside noodle-maker's stall.

CHOPSTICKS AND GOOD MANNERS

Chopsticks, or *hashi*, are mostly made of wood or bamboo. Takeaway food includes a pair of "break-apart" chopsticks, which are thrown away after use. At the meal table, chopsticks are set horizontally on a rest at each person's place. In families, each person usually has their own pair of chopsticks. They should be used in the right hand, with the rice bowl on the left. The bottom chopstick stays still, resting on the third finger, while the upper one moves, supported by the index and middle fingers, to grip and release food.
Some "don'ts" for chopsticks:
• Don't spear pieces of food.
• Don't stand chopsticks upright in food (unless for the deceased at a funeral).
• Don't put the eating end of chopsticks into the shared food dish.

◄ Formal meal of rice, soup and side dishes. Everything has its correct position in such a table setting.

▼ Western-style fast food is becoming as popular in Japan as anywhere else.

▼ In spring and summer Japanese people like to picnic outdoors.

▲ *Sushi* has become popular around the world. Vinegared sticky rice is pressed into portions, often wrapped in seaweed with *wasabi*, a hot green horseradish paste. Toppings such as raw fish are added. A *sushi* master takes many years to learn the skills of preparing *sushi*.

▼ Barbecues are uncommon. But thin slices of meat and vegetable such as eggplant, cooked over charcoal, are delicious with plum sauce.

◄ Food is delicately prepared and served with care so that it looks as good as it tastes.

EDUCATION

The standard of education in Japan is high. Children must attend elementary school for six years and junior high school for three years. They call their teachers *sensei*, which is a respectful title. The school week includes Saturday morning, as well as hours of homework. Students are also encouraged to take extra lessons after school in subjects such as calligraphy and music. Nearly all students stay for three further years at senior high school, and 40 percent go on to university or college.

▲ Senior students relaxing together.

▼ Many children start kindergarten well before the compulsory school starting age of six.

READING AND WRITING

To read Japanese, start at the top on the right of the page, and work down to the bottom left. Chinese characters, or *kanji*, were introduced to write Japanese words. Later, in order to write the many words for which no *kanji* existed, symbols for the sounds of syllables (*kana*) were added. There are two kinds of *kana*:

- *hiragana*, for native Japanese words
- *katakana*, for words which come from other languages (mostly from English).

By the time students finish high school, they are expected to have memorized the 2,000 *kanji* on the Ministry of Education "general use" list.

▲ An exchange student learns brush strokes.

▶ *Kanji* for "Australia."

▲ Tokyo University gate.

Parents often want their children to gain entry to a university, so students study hard for a place in schools with a reputation for good university entrance results. In this competitive education system, many schoolchildren attend *juku*, or afternoon cram classes. Students who are not accepted by a university at the first attempt often attend *yobiko*, or full-time cram schools.

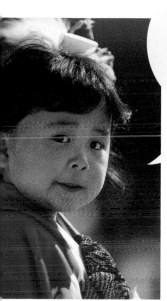

I'll spend a lot of time at school and studying. We usually attend school for 240 days a year until we are eighteen.

▶ Everyone studies the same subjects at the same level from government-approved text books. Most schoolchildren wear uniforms.

▼ Chefs in training. One of many practical areas of study available in colleges of technology for 15 to 20 year olds.

▲ Adult university courses are available.

VISITING JAPAN

Visitors to Japan can enjoy moving about easily in a safe, clean, well-organized country with an efficient transport system. There are also opportunities to absorb the unique ways of traditional thinking and living. Because few foreigners live in Japan, *gaijin* or outsiders can still arouse curiosity, especially outside the big cities. Visitors who learn some of the manners and customs will have a richer experience of the country. A good way to meet young Japanese people is through school tours or exchange programs.

▲ Wooden *kokeshi* dolls are popular with tourists.

► These students from Tocal, an Australian agricultural college, visited their sister college, Gifu, in Nagoya. The visit included home stays and working on farms, as well as playing sport and visiting cities and museums.

ACCOMMODATION

If you visit Japan, you can stay in a hotel just like one in any other country. Or you may stay in a *ryokan* or traditional inn. Here you may be met by staff wearing *kimono*. You will leave your shoes at the door and put on slippers, sit on a low chair or cushion, and have green tea and cakes. You will sleep on a floor mattress, a *futon*, which is placed on the *tatami* (floor mats made of rice straw). *Futons* are folded up and put away during the day.

► Hot baths are part of the Japanese lifestyle. A natural hot spring is called an *okutsu*. Indoors there are tubs deep enough for the water to reach your neck when sitting. You must wash and rinse yourself *before* entering the bath, keeping the bath water clean and soap-free.

◀ Hear the famous *Kodaika* drummers

▶ . . .be buried in hot volcanic sand

▼ . . .see a *karate* bout.

▲ Every season has something to offer. This is Hida Folk Village in winter.

▶ On Children's Day (May 5) carp-shaped kites are flown.

◀ Kyoto's Golden Pavilion, *Kinkaku-ji*, with gold leaf on the upper two stories. First built in the fourteenth century, it was rebuilt in 1955 after it was burned to the ground.

INDEX

How to use the Index
Words in standard type are specific references.
Words in **bold** type are general subject references;
the word itself may not appear on each page listed.

A

Ainu 12
Akihito, Emperor 26
animals 30
architecture 13, 16, 17, 18, 24, 28, 34, 35, 36, 39, 43, 45
Aso, Mount 10
atom bomb 22, 23, 24
art/s 15, 18, 19, 21, 24, 28, 34, 36

B

Bill of Rights 24
birds 9, 24, 30, 35, 45
"black ships" 20
bonsai 39
bridges 19, 27
Buddhism 14, 15, 35
Burma Railway 22
bushi 16

C

calligraphy 14, 42
cartoons 25, 37
castles 16, 18, 19
ceremonies 17, 38
China 14, 21
cities 8, 14, 18, 19, 24, 27, 34, 35, 36, 38, 39, 44
climate 8, 45
clothes 8, 12, 15, 19, 20, 34, 39, 43
craft 15
crops 30, 31
currency 9, 32
customs 8, 28, 32, 36, 38, 39, 40, 41, 44

D

daimyo 16, 18, 20
dance 16, 19, 35
democracy 26
Diet 26
dolls 15, 44

E

economy 7, 24, 27, 32, 33
Edo 18, 19, 20, 34, 36
earthquakes 10, 11, 34
education 32, 38, 42, 43
emperors 14, 16, 18, 19, 20, 21, 22, 26
emperors, Yamato 13
entertainment 19, 34, 36
Europe 17

F

family 38, 39, 40, 43
farming 8, 25, 30, 31, 38
festivals 12, 14, 16, 20, 34, 39, 45
fishing 30, 31, 38, 40
flag 13
food 17, 23, 25, 30, 31, 34, 38, 39, 40, 41, 43, 44
Fuji, Mount 9, 11, 36

G

gardens 17, 19, 29, 34, 39
geisha 19, 28
government 17, 21, 26, 27, 32

H

haiku 28
health 14, 25, 29
Heian 14, 15
Hirohito, Emperor 21, 22, 26
Hiroshima 22, 23, 24
houses 17, 29, 39

I

industry 20, 27, 28, 29, 32, 33, 36
islands 7, 8, 10

J

Jomon 12

K

kanji 14, 42
kamikaze 21
Kofun 12
Kobe 10
Korea 8, 14, 21
Kyoto 14, 15, 20, 36

L

language 9, 14, 42

M

MacArthur, General Douglas 24
manga 25, 36, 37
marriage 38
martial arts 18, 29
Meiji 20, 35
military 21, 22, 23, 24, 27
missionaries 17
money 7, 9, 32, 33, 38
mountains 8, 9, 10, 13, 17
music 14, 15, 16, 28, 36, 37, 45
myths and legends 9, 13, 16, 36

N

Nagasaki 22, 23
Nara 12, 14, 15
Nippon 13
Noh theatre 16

P

Pacific region 8, 11, 22, 24
parliament 26
Peace Constitution 24, 27
Pearl Harbor 22
poetry 11, 19, 28
population 7, 8, 9, 10, 27, 35, 39
pottery 12
puppets 18, 19

R

religion 9, 13, 14, 15, 37, 38
Ring of Fire 11
rice 12, 25, 26, 30, 31, 40, 41
rivers 9
ryokan 44

S

samurai 16, 17, 20
schools 21, 23, 42, 43, 44
sculpture 15, 21
Sea of Japan 8
seasons 8, 14, 30, 41, 45
shrines 12, 13, 34, 37
Shinto 12, 13, 14, 15, 36, 37, 38
shogun 16, 18, 19, 20
sport 18, 29, 34, 36, 37, 45
sun 13
sushi 41, 40

T

tea 17, 40, 41
technology 7, 29, 32, 33, 36
temples 17, 35
theatre 16, 18, 19, 36
tidal wave 10
Tokyo 10, 19, 20, 21, 29, 36, 38
tourism 44, 45
trade 27, 28, 29, 32, 33
transport 21, 35, 36, 44
tsunami 10

U

United States 20, 21, 22, 23, 24, 29

V

volcanoes 10, 11, 45

W

warlords 16, 18, 19, 20
western influences 7, 17, 20, 21, 28, 29, 33, 37, 41
woodcuts 10, 19
World War II 7, 21, 22, 23, 24, 34
writing 14, 42

Y

Yayoi 12
Yen 32

Z

Zen 15, 17

PICTURE CREDITS

Abbreviations: r = right, l = left, t = top, c = center, b = below

Mike Langford
Contents; Introduction; **8** bl, br; **11** bl; **13** tl, cr; **16** tl, tr, b; **17** c, bl; **18** tr, cr, bl, br; **19** tl, tr, bl; **29** tr; **30** tl, bl, br; **31** tr, c, br; **34** tl; **35** tr, c; **36** c; **37** cr; **38** tl, c, cr; **39** tl, tc, cl, b; **40** cr, bl; **41** cr; **42** tl, bl; **43** cl; **44** bl; **45** tl, tr, cl, c, b.

Japan National Tourist Organization
8 tl; **9** br; **10** tl; **12** t, bl, bc, br; **13** bl; **14** tl; **15** bl; **17** tc, cr, br; **19** br; **20** cl; **21** cr; **26** tl; **27** cl; **31** tr; **32** tl, br; **34** cr, bl; **35** br; **36** c, cr; **37** c; **40** tl; **41** tr, tl, cl; **43** tl; **44** br.

Consulate-General of Japan
11 cr, br; **14** cr, bl; **16** cr; **24** br; **26** c, cr, bl; **27** tr, cr, bl; **29** br; **32** cl, bl; **33** tr, cr, bl, br; **36** tl, br; **37** tr, cl; **39** cr, br; **42** c, **43** cr, bl, br; **45** tc.

The Japan Foundation
12 cl, cr; **15** tr, cl, br; **20** t, br; **21** tl, c, bl; **22** tl, cl, br; **23** tl, tr, cl, bl, bc, br; **24** c, bl; **25** tr, cr, c, br; **42** br.

Japan Airlines
Cover; **28** b; **34** br; **35** bl; **36** bl; **41** br; **44** cl, br.

Valerie Hill
Title; **24** tl; **29** c, bl; **37** tl; **40** br.

Ben Hill
30 c, cr; **38** bl; **41** bl; **44** cr.

Denny Allnutt
28 tl.

Canon Australia Pty Ltd
33 cl.

Kodansha International
25 Sazae-san cartoon.

National Gallery of Victoria, Melbourne
10 b.

Sony Corporation
29 tl.

Suzuki Talent Association of Australia (NSW) Inc
28 c.

Ray Sim
9 map; **11** map.

Every effort has been made to consult all relevant people and organizations. Any omissions or errors are unintentional and should be reported to Vineyard Freepress Pty Ltd.